ON BEING BLACK

Volume II

Hazel Clayton Harrison, editor
Shirley Dougan, assistant editor
Ginny Knight, artist

WITHDRAWN

 GUILD PRESS
P.O.Box 22583
Robbinsdale, MN
55422

International Standard Book Number 0-940248-40-9
Library Of Congress Catalog Card Number 81-23683
Copyright © 1991 Guild Press

CONTENTS

AFRICA: THE VISIT HOME *A traveler with a tongue does not lose the way.*

DEAR FATHER *Look to the father for the ways of the son.*

PEOPLE STILL BLEED *Thought breaks the heart.*

Introduction: *ON BEING BLACK, VOL. 2* (a history)

by Leon Knight, senior editor

In 1981, in response to an offhand, cruel and ignorant remark made during a coffee break at a conference at the University of Minnesota — "It's a pity that there are no good black writers in Minnesota" — Guild Press conducted some writing workshops, gathered submissions and published *ON BEING BLACK*, which included stories and poems by 23 writers having Minnesota connections.

We had no money and very little book-publishing experience. What we did have was a belief in ourselves as writers and editors, a conviction in the need of a small press primarily serving the needs of black and other minority writers, and an angry desire to show "them" what we could do for ourselves.

And we did it!

Hazel Clayton, the leader of the writing workshops, was the editor; Ginny Knight was the artist; and Dr. Maurice W. Britts and I assisted in any way we could. The four of us worked as an unpaid team to make the book just as good as we could.

And *ON BEING BLACK* was successful. We used the profits from the book to publish our next — and the next — and the next. Soon we had earned the reputation of being "the leading publisher of minority authors in Minnesota."

Now after ten years Guild Press is "one of the leading publishers of minority authors in the nation." *ON BEING BLACK, VOL. 2*, which is the fortieth book we have published since 1981, includes poets from 13 different states, as well as Brazil and Nigeria.

But even as things change, some things stay the same — the board members and editors are still not paid; the profits from one book are used to publish another. A younger poet who shares the Guild Press vision, Phyllis Sloan, has been added to the Board of Directors. And Hazel Clayton Harrison (who has married and moved to California since 1981) is again the editor of ON BEING BLACK, VOL. 2, and Ginny Knight (who is still married to me and living in Minnesota) is again the artist and book designer.

But, mainly, Guild Press still publishes quality anthologies of poetry and short stories. What we started with ON BEING BLACK (1981) continues with ON BEING BLACK, VOL. 2 (1991). It is a tradition we shall maintain.

Oh, Freedom

The shadow of a free man is the same as that of a slave.
African Proverb

OH, FREEDOM
(in remembrance of Dr. Martin Luther King, Jr.)
by Phyllis J. Sloan

        "Sing Hallelujah!
        Shout Ebenezer!"
The Drum Major lives on.
The marcher for all men's rights
       taught us to march.
Lived for justice.   Died for peace.
      Live for justice, die for peace:
      the birth of freedom —
           "Precious Lord, take my hand.
           Lead me on . . ."

Warrior for non-violent social change.
Follow his drum into the barricade:
      march on   sit in
      petition   demonstrate
"You must suffer with the people."
chant unity — "Peace for all mankind."
pray — "Oh, Freedom."
        "We shall overcome."

Slain martyr
      (lived for justice, died for peace)
The prophet told the truth:
      "I may not get there with you."
Now we must be keepers of his flame.
His drum beat still echoes:
       "Free at last!
       Free at last!"

If we could only follow you,
      dear Martin,
we would be   free at last!

I AM
by Antonia Apolinario

I am   strong
          resilient
          scared
          shy
          anxious
          brave
          rebellious
waiting to fly
at the edge of the cliff
          in limbo
          in ecstasy
          in laughter
          in sadness
I am   Black.

WALKIN' AND TALKIN'
by Hazel Bell

Sometimes I think
      my words have no weight
          then I remember
      my sons learned about Jesus
      from me

Sometimes I wonder
      do they ever really hear me
          then I remember
      our celebration
      on a joyous Easter Sunday

Sometimes I feel
      that satan is winning the war
          then I remember
      late night conversations
      about God's grace

Sometimes I get tired
      of doing all this talkin'
          then I remember
      I can prove it by my walkin'

SUMMER RAIN
by Thokozile Cox

dirty oceanic waves
    cross the moon
electric charges
    rent paper skies
through a jagged
    jutting-edged hole
warm torrents of rain
fall upon the arid land

my thirsty skin
    savors the rivulets
    that excite me
making me laugh
    for the pleasure
    of living

JUST DO IT
by Beverly A. Russell

do it Black folks
    do it
whether it be preachin'
    shoutin'/singin'
    buildin'/workin'
    playin'/prayin'
    politickin'
    talkin' revolution
    dancin'/prancin'
or   just restin'
whatever
    do it
and when you do it
    "do it to death"
'cause we been held back
        too long

NO SIR MISTER
by Maryetta Kelsick Boosè

No sir mister,
I ain't gonna show my teeth
and shuffle my feet —
      just cause he's in office.

I ain't gonna put away my books
and be your cook —
      just cause he's in office.

No sir mister,
I ain't gonna stay across town
and never make a sound —
      just cause he's in office.

I ain't gonna pretens I'm dead
while you plow ahead —
      just cause he's in office.

No sir mister,
I'm gonna cast my vote
and then help tote
him — right on out of office.

SAME OL' SNAKE
(Racism — 1990)
by Ginny Knight

that ol' snake is still here
wearin' a new skin
hopin' we won't recognize it
      slitherin' around
      hissin' and rattlin'
      spreadin' poison
      killin' us for
            pure wickedness
that same ol' snake

LOTTERY DREAMS
by Deborah A. Dessaso

little old black lady
        living on SSI
eating leftover's leftovers
        praying that the rent
        and the price of neckbones
        won't go up
just so she can save
        a buck to buy
        a lottery ticket
if she wins she can buy her dream —
        all the neckbones she wants
        and pay another black woman
        to cook them for her

SOUNDS OF THE CITY
(Ghetto Symphony)
by Charles E. Love

'Copter singin' overhead; sentinel of the night
Plaintive cry of a dog, somewhere out of sight
        And somewhere a man dies . . .

Po-lice car screamin' like a damn banshee
(It's cool, long as they ain't chasin' me)
        And somewhere a woman cries . . .

A quartet of cars, each one singin' out of key
Strange; no one hears this masterpiece but me
        And somewhere a child lies . . .

Choir of voices, each with a different score
Laughter of lovers to the nighttime skies outpour
        And somewhere God sighs . . .

MY NEW HOME
by Darrell Gholar

I have lived my entire life
    in the midwest
where I could walk for miles
    and miles
never having to watch my step

Now I live on the edge of the world
    California
where I can't distinguish
    sky from ocean
I must be careful not to go over
    the edge

THE CORNER
by Dennis Williams

You know
there are 27 brothers on
    that one
    corner
    all day long
i think they work in shifts
i think some spiritual force
or magnetic pull
    draws brothers
    to that corner

i know it can't be a job
    that draws brothers
    to that corner
'cause don't nobody have
    no job

i know it can't be no fine woman
    that draws all 27
    brothers to the corner
'cause ain't no fine woman
    around

i think
if these brothers were not
out holding up that corner
it just might sink into the ground!

MY SKIN IS BLACK
by Cynthia Williams

Man,
        who am I that you walk toward me
        with your back facing me?
When I open my arms
is the flame too hot?

My skin is Black
        is that your problem
        or mine?

I GOT A BIBLE AND I CAN READ
by Nancy Ellen Webb Williams

I got a Bible and I can read
What more on earth do I need?

I keeps a chicken in my pot
Ain't rich but I'm happy
        with what I got.

I got me a good workin' man.
Does the best for me he can.

I'm blessed with a roof over my head
a few sticks of furniture and a bed.

I got a daughter and a son,
two chilluns enough for anyone.

I got a burial all paid up.
It'll be there a long time
        with any luck.

I got my Jesus up in the sky
to welcome me to heaven after I die.
Yes, I got a Bible
        and I can read,
there's nothin' else anywhere
        that I need.

A THOUGHT
by Maurice W. Britts

Lord if I could do
Needed things for You,
I'd help the worn and beat
To rise above defeat.

I'd like someday to stand
As tall as any man
And pray you hear my call
For help if I should fall.

I'M NOT DONE
by Maryetta Kelsick Boosè
(Reflections on a 43rd birthday)

I'm not done
Like a river
        that flows and flows
I'm not stopping — not yet.

I've opened books for children
        words flowing from my mouth
I've stood for hours
        pushing an iron back and forth
I'm not done.

I've answered lights up and down halls
        emptied bedpans at night
sat in classrooms in the day
        so I could hang three degrees on my wall
I'm not done

I've stood in front of classrooms
        listened to children
        their joys their fears
I've seen my words of poetry
        in journals and books
and I'm still not done

Like a river that flows
        and flows
I'm not stopping — not yet.

THE CHOICE WAS TRUTH
by Nancy Ellen Webb Williams

Each word
came with its
grain of salt.

Each offering
tasted bitter.

And yet I know
the choice was Truth
and nothing else
could matter.

DR. KING DID LIVE HERE
by Gene A. Williams

Children of the quiet
        passive days
of peaceful longings
of "Bakke" ways.

There once was a little
        low man,
brown like a bronze
        statue of liberty,
he stayed among us
        a fortnight and a
                silver day.

He slept and wept
        here
helped us stand
        rainy racist weather
see through the blues
through a hell of hate
        to a heaven of hope.

Dr. King did live here.

Praise Song For Mothers

All flowers of a tree do not bear fruit.
African Proverb

PRAISE SONG FOR MOTHERS
by Layding Lumumba Kaliba

If I were a singer of songs
I'd lift my voice
        mountain high
in praise of mothers

Mothers
who scrub other people's floors
and launch their children's dreams
        on swollen knees
        and bruised knuckles

I'd take the rhythms
of Mama's pots
        and pans
and make a symphony
        of leftovers
        to feed hope
        to young dreamers

If I were a singer of songs
I'd clap my hands
and stomp my feet
raise my voice mountain high
and pull a praise song
        for mothers
from the depths of my soul

MY MILITANT GRANDMA
by Beverly A. Russell

My grandma was a militant
in her way

just like a lot of
other poor   tired
old Black folks
strugglin' along
lookin' hopeless
feeling tired/poor
and Black

they were all militant
the old folks
they would always say
"these young negroes ain't gon'
take what the old ones took"
and then (as lifted from some burden)
walk on with pride

SHE NEVER LOST A PASSENGER
by Maryetta Kelsick Boosè

They called her Harriet Tubman
and sang of the deeds she had done.
They talked of her helping her passengers
and never losing a one.

Harriet led her people to freedom
as she ran her train at night,
and risked her life for others
she fought for what was right.

Many times the going was rough
some even wanted to turn back.
But Harriet urged them ever on
her train never left the track.

12

HEAVEN
by Darrell Gholar

As a young boy,
    mother told me if I was good
    and said my prayers each night
    someday I would go to heaven.

As I lay holding you, my love
    I realize — she was right.

MAMA WAS
by Hazel Clayton Harrison

Fresh scrubbed linoleum floors
the scent of pine and vinegar
translucent windows
billowy white sheets
hanging in the sun.

Mama was
starched cotton dresses
patent leather shoes and white socks
Dixie peach meltin' between plaited hair.

Mama was
Church
the choir's sweet, soulful song
fried chicken and greens cooking
on the stove

Mama was
Thanksgiving/Easter/Christmas
all rolled into one.

THE THREE OF US
by Leon Knight

Mrs. Louise Wilcox moved slowly about her kitchen, as she always did in the morning before her bones loosened up, but more quietly than usual because her granddaughter MariLou, who was still sleeping, didn't get to stay overnight very often.

She quietly hummed as she mixed the batter for pancakes — having someone to cook for again, even for a day, was a good feeling. Thirty-five years as a cook, first at the daycare center and then at the school, were not something a person could forget easily. And Daniel — God rest his soul — loved eating. He would lean back in his chair after breakfast, pat his stomach and say, "Oh, Lou. Those pancakes were so heavy that I won't be able to cross any bridges till sundown." He would say the same thing every morning, and she loved it every time.

When she heard water running in the bathroom, she turned the burner on under the skillet. A couple of minutes later, her granddaughter, dressed in a loose, sleeveless nightgown, came in from the bedroom. "Morning, Grandma."

"Mornin', baby. You want some eggs with your 'cakes and sausages?"

"Oh, Grandma," MariLou said as she hugged her grandmother from behind, "you'll get me fat — the way you fed me last night and everything."

"Fat? You're 14 and skinny as a pole. With all the energy you burn off — what with dancin' lessons and tennis lessons and everything you're in at school — you don't have to worry about gettin' fat. At least, not yet."

"Do you think I'm too skinny, Grandma?"

"You're not too skinny — and you're not too fat. You're just right — healthy and you've got good bones. And you never did answer — do you want eggs or don't you?"

"Yeah. I'll have two — over medium." The girl pulled her nightgown tight around her and looked over her shoulder. "Grandma, do you think I'm getting any figure yet?"

Mrs. Wilcox looked lovingly at her granddaughter for a long moment. "Sure. You're gettin' some — I mean, that's not just baby fat. You've got a trim little body. I'm sure you'll be a beauty when you grow up."

"Oh, you're my Grandma. You'll think I look good, even when I weigh a ton."

Mrs. Wilcox poured another cup of coffee as MariLou started her breakfast. "Your grandfather loved his breakfast. Seems like I haven't fixed 'cakes since he passed."

MariLou laughed. "You fix me pancakes everytime I stay over, or when you come out to our place."

"And I said 'it seems like' . . . Do you know what I mean by that, baby?"

MariLou nodded. "I think so . . . I was thinking about Grandpa Dan last night. In bed there beside you — wondering what it must be like. Did you live here when Mama and Uncle George were small?"

"Yeah. Ever since your grandfather and I got married — in 1946, just after the War. Oh, that man was handsome in his uniform. He was a member of 'The Red Ball Express.' That's where he learned his drivin'. So he always had a good payin' job. That and bein' a veteran, we were able to get this house. We were about the first to buy around here — the neighborhood was just changin' over then."

The girl seemed puzzled. "Changing over?"

Mrs. Wilcox nodded, pleased with being able to teach her grandchild. "This area was all white — mostly Jewish. Some were willin' to sell to Negroes . . ."

"Negroes? Oh, Grandma, don't you mean 'Blacks'?"

"Don't interrupt your grandmother. And Negro is a perfectly good word. I can remember a time when nobody wanted to be called 'black' — it was almost as bad as bein' called 'nigger.' "

"Is that right? I didn't know that."

"Baby. There are lots of things I want you to know, but I can't tell you how glad I am that there are some things you don't have to know."

They were silent for a minute before MariLou asked, "Grandma, are you coming to my dance recital on Sunday afternoon?"

"I sure am, baby. Your mama's comin' to get me early in the mornin'. Your recital is one of the few things I'm willin' to miss church for."

"But won't you be attending service with us?"

"Oh, yeah — of course. But I meant missin' my own church." She looked at MariLou for a time before continuing: "The idea — my grandbaby studyin' ballet. And with the best teacher in the whole Twin Cities. At least, that's what your mama says."

MariLou smiled shyly before breaking into a wide grin. "Grandma, I'm the only black girl on the A-Team."

"A-Team?" Mrs. Wilcox asked, pleased with her granddaughter's pleasure.

"The recital is divided into three acts — Beginners, B-Team and A-Team. It won't say that in the program, but that's what it is. And I'm on the A-Team."

"Imagine that. My grandbaby dancin' ballet — on the A-Team."

"Actually, it's 'modern' ballet." The girl jumped to her feet, put her arms up in the classic ballet pose and did a couple of steps. "It has the ballet steps and movements, but with modern choreography."

"Ballet steps, but with modern chor-e-og-raphy." The old woman glowed with pride. "Oh, my, aren't you gettin' to be somethin'?" She held her arms out to the girl, who 'danced' over to ease herself on to her grandmother's lap.

"Do you think I'm getting too big for this, Grandma?" MariLou asked as she nestled her head into the woman's shoulder.

"You'll never be too big for this. At least, I hope not."

"Yeah." The girl snuggled contentedly against her grandmother's breast. Then she asked, "Grandma, what would you say if I told you I had a boyfriend?"

"Well, you're gettin' to that age. So it wouldn't surprise me at all. Why? Do you have one?"

"No. But I'm thinking about it." She sat up and looked at her grandmother. "But what would you 'think' about it?"

"I think your mother didn't raise a fool. None of the rest of us did either. So, when you think you've met the right boy and you think you're old enough to handle it — I think you'd do just fine. I know a lot of girls your age 'go crazy' with their boyfriends. But I don't think you would. In fact, I've been kind of surprised that you didn't have a boyfriend by this time."

"Oh, Mama freaks out whenever I even mention 'boy.' Whenever she sees an article about teenage pregnancy — especially if it mentions black and unwed mothers — she'll put it out on the kitchen table for me to read. I get so tired of statistics. I try to tell her, 'Mama, I'm not a statistic.' And she says, 'I don't want you becoming one.' It really makes me fed-up some times."

"I know, baby. But your mama is just doin' the best she can. You know, it's hard raisin' kids these days."

"Do I know? Oh, tell me about it. But, Grandma, at the senior high, they have a special program for the girls with babies. And those are white girls."

They were interrupted by a sound on the porch. Mrs. Wilcox eased MariLou off her lap and was half way to the window before a knock sounded on the door. Mrs. Wilcox peeked cautiously around the curtain. "Oh, it's just Freddie." She turned back to MariLou. "You go put a robe on, or wait in there till he's gone. We'll finish our talk later."

Mrs. Wilcox raised the shade over the window in the door before removing the chain and opening the locks. "Good mornin', Freddie. Come in."

"Morning, Mrs. Wilcox. I found your hammer. The Johnson kid had it." The young man, about 18, placed the tool on the kitchen table.

"You mean, Lionel?"

"No. The little one — Damian."

"Damian? Why he's no more than 8-years-old. Why would he steal my hammer?"

"He just saw it on your back porch and decided he wanted it. You got to be careful what you leave out, Mrs. Wilcox."

"I usually am, but I got careless this time. Thanks, Freddie."

"No problem, Mrs. Wilcox. And Damian won't bother you no more. Lionel and me told him not to mess around your place again."

He brightened up as MariLou, wrapped in her long robe, came in. Mrs. Wilcox said, "Freddie, this is my 'granddaughter.' MariLou, this is Freddie."

"Well, good morning to you, 'granddaughter' of Mrs. Wilcox."

MariLou blushed and said, "Hi."

"Freddie," Mrs. Wilcox asked, "will you be goin' by the library?"

"For you, the 'grandmother' of MariLou, I can go most anywhere. What do you need, Mrs. Wilcox?"

"I have a couple of books to return."

"My pleasure, It will be no trouble at all."

As Mrs. Wilcox got the books from the living room, Freddie said to MariLou, "I play drums for 'Spontaneous Combustion.' Ever hear of us?"

MariLou shook her head.

"We're kinda big in the area. Come and hear us sometime, and I'll introduce you around."

"Okay," MariLou said softly.

"Here are the books, Freddie," Mrs. Wilcox said as she returned to the kitchen. "You're sure it's no bother."

"No bother at all," Freddie said. "Well, I better be shufflin' off." And, for MariLou's benefit, he did a Michael Jackson 'moon walk' to the door, spun around once and was gone.

MariLou looked at her grandmother and started giggling. "Grandma, who is that boy?"

"Evidently a boy who likes you," Mrs. Wilcox teased.

"Where does he go to school?"

"He dropped out a couple of years ago. He's mentioned joinin' the navy, if he can't get a decent job pretty soon."

MariLou frowned. "Oh, darn. A drop-out." She flicked her hand through the air. "Well, so much for Freddie."

"What do you mean by that."

MariLou sighed. "I don't have time to be interested in a 'drop-out.' Any boy for me has to plan on going to college — at least." Suddenly she stiffened and cocked her head to listen. "Mama's coming."

Mrs. Wilcox looked at the clock. "Your mama already?"

"Yeah. I can tell the sound of her car."

Then Mrs. Wilcox heard it too — the high-pitched sound of the diesel-engine as a car pulled to a stop in front of the house. A few seconds later, the rapid "clack-clack" of high-heeled shoes sounded on the sidewalk leading to the kitchen porch. Mrs. Wilcox opened the door before her daughter could knock. "Good mornin', Brenda. You're a bit early, aren't you?"

"Morning, Mama. I was feeling 'antsy' so I left as soon as I could." She looked at MariLou. "Girl, who was that I saw coming out of the house?"

"It was just a boy, Mama."

"I know it was a boy. But what boy?"

"That was Freddie," Mrs. Wilcox said. "He came by to see me — to take some books back to the library for me."

Brenda looked first at her mother and then at her daughter.

"Well, okay." Then she held out her arms to hug her mother. "Good morning, Mama." Then she turned to MariLou. "You too, girl."

"Good morning, Mama," MariLou said, returning the hug. "I didn't know you'd be here so soon. I'll hurry and get my things packed."

"No hurry, girl. I'm early and I need to talk to your grandmother anyway."

Mrs. Wilcox poured her daughter a cup of coffee and got out the milk as MariLou headed for the bedroom. "I don't have any nutrasweet," she said.

"Oh, sugar won't hurt me once in a while," Brenda said. She sighed heavily as she poured the milk into the coffee.

"Didn't you have a good time at the banquet last night?" Mrs. Wilcox asked.

"Actually, it was a going-away party for someone who got promoted to the company headquarters in Houston. That went fine. But I really got bummed out at work yesterday."

"Let me fix you some cakes as you tell me about it. The batter's right here."

"Oh, no," Brenda began, and then weakened. "Well, okay. Just a couple."

Mrs. Wilcox smiled as she whipped up the batter again and turned on the stove. "Well, what happened?" she asked.

"I had to fire someone yesterday. I know it's part of my job. But I think I got used."

"Why do you say that?"

"It was a young black woman. A single mother. Several men could have told her but, no, they tapped good-old-black-woman Brenda to be the hatchet man. She really told me off."

"Told you off?" Mrs. Wilcox repeated.

"She called me a lot of names — including some I haven't heard in a long time. But what could I do, Mama? She missed too many days — was late the rest of the time — and didn't get her work done when she was there. She just wasn't working out. And other workers are willing to carry someone only so far."

Mrs. Wilcox sat down again as she placed a plate of pancakes before her daughter. "Those things happen, dear. As you said, it's part of your job. You'll feel better after you eat."

"She said I didn't remember who I was or where I came from — that I didn't have any sympathy for anyone else who is trying to better herself. She said nothing has changed for 'real' people like herself except that it's now 'Oreos' like me — white niggers— who are standing on her head. She called me an 'Uncle Tom' — doing the white man's dirty work."

"Oh, don't pay any attention to what someone like that says."

"But, Mama, what if it's true?"

"It's not true. And she better not let me hear . . ."

Brenda interrupted. "She called me an 'educated fool.' Mama, what if I am?"

"At least you're educated."

In spite of herself, Brenda started laughing. "Oh, Mama. What would I do without you? 'At least I'm educated.'"

Mrs. Wilcox didn't share in the laughter. "I'm not jokin' about this, Brenda. Fools like that really make me mad. A lot of people worked hard to clear the field and to break the first sod. And then some fool like that comes along who won't even till her own garden. She wants to blame 'Uncle Tom' when she goes hungry. It's people like that who are really betrayin' the dream. Not you. A lot of people struggled long — and some died — to open doors for us. And your daddy and I worked hard so your brother and you could have the chance to do things we never could do. So don't let a fool like that make you feel guilty."

Brenda smiled shyly at her mother and nodded. "I don't know why I was ever so lucky to have such a wise woman for my mama. You're right, of course — just like you always are." She leaned back in her chair. "I knew I had good reason to come early." Then she leaned forward again. "Mama, why don't you come out to live with us? That area on the 'walk-out' level can easily make a nice little apartment for you. I know MariLou would love it. And I really worry about you staying much longer in this neighborhood."

Mrs. Wilcox shook her head. "How many times do I have to say it — this is my home. I'm just two blocks from church — and they really need me when they have church dinners and functions. Besides, I have my work at the daycare center."

"That's just volunteer work — you can do the same at a daycare near us."

"This is a 'special needs' center. Henrietta Hawkins' daughter Evelyn runs it. Some of those babies need an old woman like me to just hold them because they get abused at home."

"But the news reports say that the county takes babies out of homes like that now."

"Well, Evelyn reports a lot of abuse that the county does nothin' about. So I try to help her out as best I can. I need to be here to go hug those babies. I may be in my sixties and retired, but I can still be of some use."

"Yeah, I know. But, sometimes I need you too — like today. And sometimes I do need help with MariLou."

Mrs. Wilcox extended her hand to pat her daughter's arm. "No, you don't."

Puzzled, Brenda looked at her mother. "Mama?"

Mrs. Wilcox smiled gently. "Sometimes you don't realize what a good job you've done raisin' that girl. You don't need any help at all."

Brenda smiled her appreciation. "I still would like you to come and live with us. When I think of all you and Daddy did for me, I want to do something for you now."

"Well, there is one thing that you can do for me."

"Anything. Just name it."

"Let MariLou come to stay with me more often."

When Brenda inhaled sharply, Mrs. Wilcox pressed on: "I know you don't like her bein' in this neighborhood very much — and I'm glad she doesn't have to go to school here — but this is where you grew up. And she'd be with me all of the time."

Brenda sighed, "Oh, Mama." Then she called, "MariLou."

MariLou's hair was half combed when she stuck her head into the kitchen. "Mama?"

"Since there are just teachers' conferences at school today, how would you like to stay with your grandmother?"

The girl's eyes sparkled. "Oh, can I, Mama?"

"I have a late meeting. So I'll pick you up about 6:45."

"Thanks, Mama," MariLou said, before disappearing back into the bathroom.

"Can you come for supper?" Mrs. Wilcox asked.

"No, but I will bring dessert, if that's all right? I'll phone John, and we can go out later to get something. But for early dessert, it's just the three of us. Okay?"

"That sounds fine — just the three of us."

MISSISSIPPI MAMAS
by Phyllis J. Sloan

for older ladies
            descended from southern places
with peach-cobbler smiles
and adoring praline eyes
            who say   "how do?"
            and greet us others
as "baby" "honey" "dear" and "sweetheart"
you'll never know how many times
            your endearments warm me
while in your stores/cleaners/restaurants
            and homes
Missouri, Chicago, New Orleans, Alabama
            Mississippi Mamas

sometimes i'm yours
when just being mine
            is not enough

Black Doll

A bird walking nevertheless has wings.
African Proverb

BLACK DOLL
by Bernard V. Finney, Jr.

Black doll, sittin' on a shelf at the
      county fair,
you do not have a face.
      the other dolls have faces — they
      sing and move their arms.

My Black memories hurt
      when I see you without a face.
My mother's mother
      was without a face
      while pickin' cotton,
      plantin' beans and bleedin'
      from the master's whip.

Black doll I want you
      to see beauty
      hear hummingbirds
            and speak
though faceless
      you will be heard
      and the earth shall tremble!

THE HISTORY LESSON
by Hazel Clayton Harrison

"Boys and Girls," Miss Bell rapped her ruler sharply on the edge of her desk, "May I have your attention? Today we will discuss the Discovery of America. Please turn to page ten of your history books."

The children suddenly stopped talking and began opening their desks, taking their books out, and flipping through pages.

Miss Bell gave them a few minutes to find the right page. Then she cleared her throat. "Now who can tell me who discovered America?" she asked.

Ten hands shot up. Miss Bell's eyes circled the room. They were a fine group of students. There was little Amy Madigan. Her father owned Madigan's Furniture store. Fred Holiday's mother was a nurse and his father sold real estate. Jenny Carson's father was an attorney and her mother worked as a teacher. The only child who did not seem to fit was Calvin Wicks, the only Black child in the class. Poor Calvin. What an ugly child he was. Dark, dark skin. So dark, at night all you could see were his eyes. A rather odd shaped head. Thick lips. Miss Bell abhorred stereotypes. Her mother was Jewish and had told her about the discrimination and racism she faced during World War Two. But even she had a problem with Calvin's looks. He reminded her of the watermelon eating Black children on those old posters of the South. Still, she tried to overcome her own prejudices and treat Calvin just like all the other children.

Usually, Calvin sat quietly in the back of the room. But this time his hand was among those that were raised. Delighted that he knew the answer to her question, she called his name.

"Stand up Calvin, so we can all hear you," she said.

Calvin stood up. "The Indians," he said loudly.

Giggles and laughter rippled through the room.

Miss Bell ordered the children to be quiet then turned to Calvin. "Why Calvin, where did you hear such a thing?" she asked. "Everyone knows who discovered America. Can someone else tell us?"

This time she chose Amy who proudly gave the correct answer.

Embarrassed, Calvin slid back into his seat and hung his head as the children sneered at him.

Throughout the rest of the day, Miss Bell noticed that he paid no attention to the lessons. Instead, he stared out the window, daydreaming.

Not wanting to embarrass him further by reprimanding him in front of the other children, she decided that she would speak to him at the end of the day. When the last period ended, she called him to her desk.

"Calvin, why didn't you read your homework assignment last night?" she asked, a look of concern on her powdered white face.

"I did Ma'am," Calvin replied, sincerely.

"But how could you have and not known who discovered America?"

"'Cause my daddy told me that the Indians discovered America. They was here before Columbus got here. So they must have discovered it first."

Miss Bell thought for a moment. She did not know what to say. Of course she knew the Indians were here first, but as far as she was concerned there was only one interpretation of American History — the one in the Houghton Mifflin text.

"The fact that the Indians were here first is not important," she said. "What is important is that Columbus sailed all the way from Spain and found them. Do you understand?"

Calvin nodded his head, but there was a puzzled look on his face. Miss Bell knew he did not fully understand. Perhaps the concept was beyond his comprehension. Why, she wondered was his father telling him another version of history. He was probably an uneducated man. Feeling that it would do no good to talk to Calvin further; she dismissed him and turned to the mound of papers on her desk that needed correcting.

For the next few weeks Calvin sat quietly in the back of the room, daydreaming or looking out the window. Then one day the subject of the day's history lesson was that curious period of American history known as the Slavery Era. Miss Bell had read the student's stories about how the slaves were brought from Africa and were later freed when Abraham Lincoln signed the Emancipation Proclamation. So she was sure even Calvin knew the correct answer to the question she was about to ask.

"Calvin," she said, "why don't you tell us who freed the slaves."

Her question obviously caught Calvin, who had been thinking about the softball game he was going to play after school, by surprise. Slowly, he stood up.

"Hmmmm." He searched for an answer in the back of his mind. Then suddenly his face brightened like a shining piece of black coral. "Harriet Tubman," he said, proudly.

The class pealed with laughter. Miss Bell rapped her ruler on her desk and turned to Calvin, a vein popping out on her neck.

"That is incorrect," she said. "have you been listening to anything we have studied in this book so far?" she glared at him.

Calvin's head dropped. "Yes Ma'am," he said, "but my daddy told me Harriet Tubman freed the slaves, too."

"Your father is a mechanic, not a history teacher. And since you cannot seem to get your history lessons straight, you will stay after school today." Miss Bell punctuated her remarks by having the entire class turn to the chapter on Abraham Lincoln and reread it.

After class Miss Bell made Calvin write on the board one hundred times that Columbus discovered America in 1492 and Abraham Lincoln freed the slaves in 1863. She was going to make sure that he learned those facts if he learned nothing else.

Calvin had written half way across the board when a tall, dark, bearded man wearing a pair of grease stained overalls appeared in the door.

Although she had never met him, Miss Bell knew right away that he was Calvin's father.

"I came to pick up my son," he said, rather sheepishly, holding his hat in his hand.

Glad to have the opportunity to talk to him about the problems she was having with Calvin; Miss Bell stood up and walked over to him, her hand extended.

"You must be Mr. Wicks," she said, "I'm Calvin's teacher and I have been meaning to speak to you or your wife about some problems we've been having with him. Would you please step out in the hall with me."

Mr. Wick's eyebrows knitted and he looked at Calvin out of the corner of his eye.

"Exactly what is the problem?" he asked when they were standing in the empty hall.

"It's his American history lessons. He says you are teaching him some things about history that, quite frankly, are not in our textbooks. I realize Black History is important, but in the Public Schools he must learn the correct history."

Suddenly Mr. Wicks' eyes clouded. He glared at her. "Black History is the correct history," he roared, "I teach my boy the truth. I teach him what he needs to know to survive in this world. I teach him how to be a man. He can't be no man running around here believing that Black folks never did nothing but pick cotton. I seen what you got him writing on the board in there. Columbus discovered America. That's a bunch of garbage if you ask me. That's just history the way white folks wrote it. I teach him the way Black folks wrote it. Now if you'll excuse me, I'm taking my boy home."

Miss Bell just stood there, her face ash white, her hands shaking like feathers. She said nothing as Mr. Wicks ushered Calvin out the door.

The next day, Calvin's seat in the back of Miss Bell's room was empty. When Miss Bell asked the principal about him, he told her that Calvin's mother had filled out papers for him to transfer back to their neighborhood school.

Such a pity, Miss Bell thought, as she went back to her class to prepare the lesson plans for the next week. No wonder so many Black children never finished school.

MOTHER'S ADVICE
by Doris L. Pruitt

> Listen my daughter — get this perfectly clear,
> and to this advice for dear life adhere.

Allow yourself the opportunity,
to reach your full maturity.
Don't bring a child into this world,
while you're still a little girl.
Don't be easy or be labeled a tramp,
don't allow your name to have that cruel stamp.
When you are carefree and in your teens,
you won't know how to soothe a baby's screams.

Let your mind overrule your heart,
don't be stupid play it real smart.
No matter how handsome or sweet his voice,
don't let him take advantage, make the right choice.
If you bear a child, the duty is yours
can you handle dirty diapers, bottles and chores?

Before I'm a grandma, I'd better be old,
now you can't say you've never been told.
If following your own mind you hard-headedly insist
please take this advice from a true realist.

> If you go against my advice of your own free will,
> then we need to talk about the birth control pill.
> Though you may not think much of this rhyme,
> your mother's just begging you to
> > give yourself time.

WRAPPED IN SORROW
by Ginny Knight

a mistake
her life began
     wrapped in sorrow
     an unwanted child

she will always carry
that burden
     like some disease
     infesting her soul
     a throw-away child
     sorrow-wrapped
          rejected before
          begun

FOR DEBORAH
From Yesterday
by Phyllis J. Sloan

your arms are folded little girl
     holding yourself together
and we are wading in your vomit
while i ask your mother's phone number
you think   and then recite it
     stating "she won't come"
     "i live with my boyfriend
     he's the one with the letter jacket on
     is he out there? his name is jeffery
         is he out there?"

you are sick and weak and eighteen
a little girl   though eighteen
we are standing in what may be
the symptom of your own child
     i don't see your jeffery: brother   father   lover
is your address a home?

i have not met you before now
but   i understand your folded arms
little girl
     holding yourself together

I HAVE A TOY I CAN'T RETURN
by Alma Curry

15 and pregnant
        I'll be the center of attention
        married (he did say he loved me)
        now I will have
                something   to call my own
                      to play with to love me
suddenly he's gone
        I don't know what to do
        didn't he say he loved me?
              he told me he was sterile too

labor was long and hard
        I got so tired
            it was worth it 'cause
            baby is cute just a little doll
but baby dolls were easy
        baby dolls were fun
            dolls don't need food
            don't get sick and cry
for a real live baby
        there are so many things I lack
        but   this is a toy
        I can't give back

LITTLE GIRL YOU SCARE ME
by Leon Knight

Little girl, you scare me.
I don't like seeing you die
when your mama lets you starve
        on "mother's day"
'cause one of your fathers
stops by for a night or two.
        All weekend,
they drink   next month's milk,
               next week's love.
It's all gone —   nothing's left for you.
        Little girl, you scare me —
        I don't like watching you die.

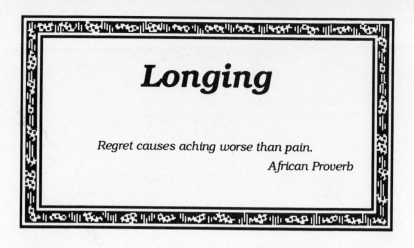

Longing

Regret causes aching worse than pain.

African Proverb

LONGING
by Elizabeth I. Roberts

Keeping still I watch
      as the kitten times
her movements towards
         me.
      (She misses her mother's
      sweet milk.)

She feels warm and soft
         against me.
The longing to be touched
      purrs within us.

WARM GLOW
By Phyllis J. Sloan

your face
        like a burgandy-black
        mahogany tiki
fills my palms with pleasure
— what a well crafted brow!

i've always been so fond
of wood
its rich earthen glow
        skilled edges

so much is veneer these days
        i cannot help but
        hold you
        close

QUIET LOVE
by Charles E. Love

I speak a quiet love to you,
My heart's gift to you only.
It comes not as a tempest, but
As night wind,
        soft and lonely.

I whisper this passion felt
Into your waiting ear.
I speak of it quietly,
So no one else will hear.

Some shout of love so urgently
Into the skies above,
But my words to you float gently.
Mine is
        a quiet love.

MARY'S GLORY
by Nancy Ellen Webb Williams

Mary'd only
wash her hair
in rain-barrel water,
cause rain-barrel water
wasn't alkali hard.

Then she'd give
her crownin' glory
a vinegar rinse,
and dry it
with sunshine
at the side
of the yard.

LOVE EQUATION
by Hazel Clayton Harrison

math was simple then

you plus me equalled one
with you, i became whole
i understood the meaning
of Yin and Yang,
cause and effect,
earth and sky
don't good things come in pairs?

then you left
just when i thought i had
it all figured out

now
two minus one
equals
nothing
no matter how many times
i subtract

THE DATE
by Charlene Higginbotham

I shoved into the box the sound of me.
The scream,
      with its tongue curled up,
The hand growing claws,
My fur,
      bristling in moonlight.
I gnawed on meat of old bones.
Finally,
      sweeping the dry forearms,
      the ragged femurs,
      under the sofa.
I dressed my haunches in silk and wool,
and formed my tits to breasts in gauzy lace.
Candles I lit,
      dimming the glint in my eyes,
      hiding the savage lust.
And when at last his sound came to my door,
      I opened and there,
      with daffodils he stood,
unsuspecting.

COOL CATS: A VIEW
by Beatrice Julian

You must tell all cats facing you,
That tickling is not permittted
That teasing whiskers are not allowed
Or shrill or simpering meows
Or slashing with uncut claws.
You must tell all cats facing you
That you are wise to gold flecked almond eyes
That you know alley ways, carpeted corridors,
Tile, brick, hardwood, plank and even sinking sand,
Tell them cats you know, that you know
And will not answer their demands

REMEMBRANCES
by Shirley Dougan

he reminds me of   the sixties
a time of Temptations   and Miracles
a time of hope   and dreams.

I didn't know him then   yet,
when I think of those times
        my thoughts return
        to him.

AT THE BEACH
by George D. Clabon

Sitting high on the rock
We watched the white waves rise
Reach for the sky and settle on the beach
As the young surfers
So graceful on their flying boards
Tried to ride the big one for thrills and spills

Sitting high on the rock
Hotdogs steaming on the cart
Fresh seafood—lobster, crab, flounder, et al
Stroked my nostrils with soft affection
Dining at Tony's on the Pier
With the pigeons and seagulls

Sitting high on the rock
As he caressed the keys gently
The sensuous, sexy, sax responded
To deliver Hank's enrapturing melody
While Tom Collins and Napoleon arrived
Bringing spirit to the night

Sitting on the rock
As we enjoyed the setting sun
The painting unfolded on the canvas
As nature applied the brushes
To create memories to treasure
When the sunset marked the day

I BET THEY'RE STILL DANCIN'
by Layding Lumumba Kaliba

sometimes midnight finds me starin'
out my bedroom window embracin'
the vastness of the evening sky
tryin' to keep time to jazzglow move
ments and rhythm brilliance
like a moon-eyed boy peekin' in an
all night ballroom i'm raptured by
the magnificence of star studded ladies
and galactic gents, blood pulsating to
juke joint foot stompin'
       i bet mama and daddy are at the jam
they always loved to dance, mama's probably
wearing a sequined gown made of
rainbow lace illuminated by daddy's
broad smile wrapped around
the enchantment of majestic motion
       i bet they're still dancin'
mama swingin' and swayin', daddy pullin'
cloud soft splits, Count Duke sharin'
center stage, Billie and Dinah on the mike

i bet The Heaven Palace Ballroom
is jumpin'; oh! i can see it so clearly now
and i know the rest of the family
is watchin' too from their windows,
caught up on every move, just like old times
       i know they're still dancin'
and Sam Cooke is croonin'; Jackie
Wilson's shoo be do be do woppin', Nat King
Cole ticklin' the keys, Bessie beltin' blues
and children starin' out their
windows watchin' the moonlight Jam

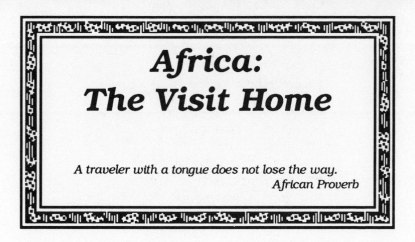

Africa:
The Visit Home

A traveler with a tongue does not lose the way.
African Proverb

AFRICA: THE VISIT HOME
by Hazel Bell

Never dreamed I'd visit my beginnings
had no thought of ever seeing where I came from

Then I heard the drums
and felt the pulsing answer
        from my heart

My ancestors from both shores
        now hold me close

COUNTING
by Beatrice Julian

Millions
in the homelands make a
small number
        while thousands
on white streets
of black misery
lift freedom appellations
        by the hundreds
choked in the swill of new cities
        ten workdays
        fill a week of seven
for   one man
        one group
        one decision
Afrikaners count
Africans do not

HAIL MANDELA
by Connee Chivers-Bowman

They freed you from prison.
        But you were already free
        As your soul and spirit
                Took mighty flight
        In what you thought was right.

Behind cold iron bars
        You held steady
        But your message escaped
        The world felt your vibrations
                Unshakeable
                Undefeated
                Undaunted

Hail Mandela
        On the way to being free!

I MUST GO TO NAIROBI
by Elizabeth I. Roberts

The conference begins with women,
      rich and poor,
      dark skin to palest light.
The Nairobi air breathes
and   speaks with different voices
        about survival.
      Some women come with empty bowls;
      some bring their minds and bodies
      still showing the mark of chains.
In the small space of shade stand women
carrying their silence like stones.

I walk many miles from a small village
where firewood and dreams are scarce.
      I'm made worthy
by the number of babies I have
and how well I rekindle the ashes for cooking.

Stones along the journey cut my feet
and the dry heat burns like smoke in my nostrils.
      I beat a drum while walking.
      The tightly pulled skin
      is made from tales
         told by women of the village
         who weep in the night.

I must go to Nairobi
      to tell other women
      living in dryness,
      silence and famine
         there is a song.

HIDEBOUND

by Chema Ude

the cause is skin-deep
they love the land
       they pain to keep
their very own nativeland
what else is there to do?

they sweat-soak the diamond and gold
       to glitter
that stocks bull markets
and chokers the necks and wrists
of men and women
in lofty anticeptic places;
       places where caviar
drowned with chateau blanc
insulates exploitive consciences
from human corrals in Transvaal
       shantytowns of
       Basutoland and Johannesburg

they love the land
       they try to own
held in stagnant foreign hands
their very own fatherland
as omnipotent Tixo watches on
and the titihoyas chorus their
       larkish indifferent freedom lullabies
what else is there to do?

until the velds are set ablaze
with scarlet rivers of crushed lilies drowned
and cleansed in frenzied joyous feasts
to end their long denied uhuru victory
       for their motherland

whatever else
is there to do?

WE HAVE ALWAYS LIVED HERE
(forced relocation to a Black "homeland", South Africa)
by Ginny Knight

I was born here
        and my mother
        and my father
                and their mothers
                and their fathers
it seems we have
always lived here

how can we leave this place
we have known so long
        where we know the stars
                so even in the darkness
                we can find our way
        where every tree
                marks our time
                        and place

how can we leave the place where
        Grandmother was born
        and died
        where Grandfather told us stories
                around the fire
        and Jabulani herded
                the finest cattle ever seen

must we now be herded onto trucks
so crowded we cannot carry
        mama's favorite cooking pot
must Tandi leave behind
        her favorite toy
and Justice leave his love
        as if it were mere foolishness

must we leave this place
where it seems
we have always lived

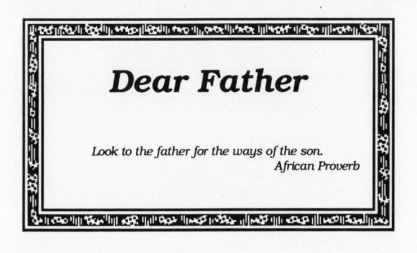

Dear Father

Look to the father for the ways of the son.
African Proverb

DEAR FATHER
by Hazel Clayton Harrison

I have seen your burdens
carried like an ox
     carries bundles
     of hay, wood and bricks.
I have seen you in the fields,
     in the mines, in the mills,
Seen the sweat flow
from your brow like muddied rivers,
seen your bloodied hands,
the fire and rain in your eyes,
and now
     the dying embers.
I have seen your burdens
carried like an ox
     carries bundles
     of hay, wood and bricks.

CHICAGO AND FRANKLIN
By Richard F. Gillum

Every day I see the same
Indians on crutches
Limping into a liquor store.
I am like them.
An elderly Negro drives by
Sitting poker straight
In a black Chrysler.
I loosen my tie
And slouch on the bus.
The world is full of lame people.
My handwriting on the bus
Looks just like my father's
Just before he died.

FOR OLD MEN
By Phyllis J. Sloan

for old men
        with sly smiles
and sweet winks

who breakfast at the same place
        to ensure themselves good service
        by entertaining the same waitresses
                tipping high
                cajoling higher
who in their flirtatious manner
        compliment all women

we miss them
        when they're gone
each in his own time
        leaving the counter one day
        never to return

WINDS OF CHANGE
by George D. Clabon

the construction crew
went about their business
building a Kroger's store
across the street
I sat on the bottom step
and listened to the old man
Mr. Norris
I never knew his age
but I considered him wise
he talked of times
changing faster than he

it was only yesterday
to him
neighborhoods had pride
dwellings did not stretch
skyward
to become projects
where people
reside like ants
on top of each other
venting their frustration
on their brethren
in a futile attempt
to halt
the winds of change

as we played cork ball
similiar to the stick ball
played in Harlem
or so I'm told
I reflected on his words
tried to see my future
in the new era
while the beliefs I learned from
my ancestors
whirled around me
blown by
the winds of change

MOVING DAY
by Richard F. Gillum

"Frank! Frank! You gone to sleep in that shed? I want us to get to Emporia before dark."

"I'm comin', Jenny. I don't want to be leavin' nothin' I might need in town," Frank replied with irritation.

He led their milk cow out of the shed and tied her to the back of the wagon. He seemed to have shrunk inside his faded overalls, and his gait lacked its usual crisp quickness. His nut brown face was drawn as he adjusted the furniture, rolls of bedding, boxes of pots and pans, and their remaining supplies. As he jerked on the ropes holding the load, he gazed over the wagon at the fields with their brown autumn stubble. He thought back to June of 1879 when he had first set eyes on this homestead.

Fresh out of the Ninth Cavalry he had ridden up the Santa Fe Trail from New Mexico to find a home in the Free State of Kansas. A white preacher in Council Grove had told him of the homestead colony of blacks founded by old Pap Singleton at Dunlap. He had heard neither of Singleton, who had been helping blacks from Tennessee move to Kansas for years, nor of the frenzied exodus of blacks from Louisiana, Mississippi and Texas who fled white bulldozing and starvation wages in the spring of '79.

When he arrived at Dunlap, he found families camping in the open, in makeshift tents or under wagons. At first it seemed a colorful scene. Women in long homespun dresses tending the fires or carrying water from the river, small children sleeping on quilts on the ground, or running among the women. Then he realized many families had neither teams, plows, supplies, nor money to buy them. Most of the men were off looking for work at nearby farms.

Good land sold for six dollars an acre. He had been lucky arriving with his horse, and nearly $200 in an old sock in his pocket. Within days he had scouted out this homestead, set up camp, bought a harness and plow and set to work getting in a crop of corn. The crop did well and besides tending it he was able to scythe enough prairie grass for a winter's worth of hay. He put up a one-room shack and a lean-to for the horse and bought a few chickens.

The winter of '79-'80 was mild. He found time from his work to ride around and meet his neighbors. That was how he met Jenny. She had come west with her sister and brother-in-law from Davidson County, Tennessee. Jenny had two children, Dinah and Buddy, by a man who had run off and left her. Given the dearth of eligible women, the prospect of a ready-made family did not deter Frank from calling on her steadily through the winter and marrying her in the spring of '80.

The next six seasons had been good ones by dent of hard work, and favorable land, weather and prices. Frank enlarged the house to four rooms as his family expanded by three.

Then the rains failed and crops were scanty. Farmers were hit hard and there was talk of a depression in the towns. Jenny had never liked the harsh realities of homesteading. Although she worked hard on their farm, she regularly let Frank know that she thought they would be better off in town where, in addition to his earnings, she could be paid by whites for the nursing and midwife services she often rendered free or for a few bartered goods to their indigent farm neighbors. She also wanted schooling for the children.

While times were good, Frank put her off with talk of improvements to the house and a few months of part-time school in Dunlap for Dinah and Buddy. But after the second crop failure, he could resist no longer, he rode to Emporia to find work.

After three weeks he had the promise of a job as a gardener and houseboy for a well-to-do white family, an offer for his farm at two dollars an acre, and he found an affordable house to rent.

The last yellow leaves of the cottonwoods along the Neosho were falling as he rode back up the river with the good news. Frank's initial flush of excitement at his unexpected success in town had left him by the time he had covered the nearly twenty miles to the homestead. He took care of his horse before going slowly to the house to give Jenny the news. When the children's excited greetings and queries about candy and presents subsided he stated in a matter of fact way, "Found a job in town and a place to move to. I can get something for the farm too."

"That's wonderful," Jenny beamed, "isn't it children? We can live in a town with stores, and a school, and streets, and a church." She hugged each of the children and than turned to Frank. "You don't seem happy about the good news," she said noting his limp response and emotionless face.

"Oh, I'm happy all right. It'll be fine for you and the kids."

"I suppose you'd rather stay on this damn farm and starve."

"I never said that. I said I'm happy. We'll leave in a couple of days and you'll never have to set eyes on this place again. That's what you want, ain't it? So just let me be."

He snatched up his hat and stalked out of the house. He headed by habit for the fields.

Frank said little at supper or the next day as they boxed the little store of goods accumulated over the past eight years. It didn't seem like much to show for the back-aching, brow-sweating toil. But the land was his, his to farm in any way he pleased. If only the rains had returned this year. Maybe he could have hung on to his dream of building the place up, expanding even when Buddy and little Joshua grew old enough to work at his side. Then he would have something fine to pass on to them and their children. But no, it couldn't be.

"You gonna stand there gazin' off into space all mornin'?" Jenny snapped, impatient to be underway.

"Alright, alright. I'm just thinking of what I might be leavin'."

He turned from the wagon and went back to the house for one final check. He looked fondly at the rough board walls and swept dirt floor, after hesitating a moment, he stepped inside.

Jenny had put the children in the wagon, and now as Frank lingered in the house, they wanted down again. After forbidding them to move, she stalked to the door, hands on hips, to ferret Frank out and get him going. Looking in the door she saw him standing in the center of the room, head down shoulders shaking. She approached slowly, wondering if he was sick. As she reached his side she saw he was crying.

Aware of her presence, he said huskily, "I'm going to miss this old place."

Jenny stood still not knowing what to say.

As if coming to himself, Frank wiped his face brusquely on his sleeve, put his arm around her shoulders and hurried her towards the door.

MY FATHER'S HOUSE

(for C.R. Dougan)
by Shirley Dougan

My father's house is a place
with   a private key —
the doors to my Father's house,
                though closed tight
are opened   with love.

The spirit of his house
is one of truth.
                Quiet laughter
rings through the rooms.

Love,   truth
and   the spirit of love
make me know
                God lives
in my father's house.

DADDY
by Ginny Knight

Daddy came home
    once
that I remember

his presence
    filled
the tiny house —
the screaming
    and fighting
shook the walls
    like a wind storm

we watched with
    sideways glances
afraid to look at him
    directly

when he left it was as if
we had been holding
    our breath
and life went back to normal

years later I was called
to his bedside   as he lay
    dying

I couldn't comprehend
    that small
    shrunken figure

from that visit
so many years before —
his visit that had
so overwhelmed us
    those few days
I had thought he was
    a big man

WHERE'S PAPA
by Shirley Dougan

so many women
so many children
papa comes
      once
baby comes
papa's gone

so many women
so many children
but
     where's papa

DADDY DIDN'T COME
by Bobby D. Cobbs

Mother came home late last night
from the white folk's kitchen
     we had left overs

Irene dressed
     and undressed the table

Oscar wiped his greasy mouth
     then belched

Joyce got sick
     went to bed

John, the youngest whimpered
     as he sucked mother's breast

I was full as a tick
     rubbed my belly

daddy didn't come
     daddy didn't come

People Still Bleed

Thought breaks the heart.

African Proverb

PEOPLE STILL BLEED
by Leon Knight

People still bleed
        in South Africa.
In Nicaragua children
        still starve.
Raging fires
have not been put out
        in Harlem or Watts —
or on the near-northside.

Rich sauces and creams
in   The Executive Dining Room
are made of cheese taken
from the tables of the poor
        and weak.

Nothing has changed
(and my beard grows gray) —
        Howard Beach, New York
        Forsyth County, Georgia
The White House, Washington D.C.
(Isn't that building aptly named?)

And in South Africa
        people still bleed.

DOWNSTREAM
by Errol Miller

There has been a change
in Joe's wonderful sleepy eyes
begging your pardon, Joe
you flow exotic into this
one last poem of you unhampered
by the shadows on your trail at night
    lonely as Chicago's masses
I have seen you huddling in the stockyards
shredding flesh and bone, milking white stars
I am astounded by the knives that touch you
in the translucent glow of a lifetime much too old
        why doesn't God comfort you more
there is no wisdom in the soft thighs of women
an American myth it was of muscle-men
and immortality lying down together
        in impulsive acts
            as moths flapped away delirious
I am searching for a pardon for you
among my Southern souvenirs
        the language troubles me
the weight of the River Jordan
and the roar of the crowd from Shangri-La
soon you will explore darker waters
parting the reeds just below Pittsburgh
        you'll yearn for deliverance
            another drink of strong rye whiskey
touching both sides of two worlds
at the crossing a ferry boat
is looking for a few good men
        I can't tell you about downstream
you must simply hold the arrow
as it quivers into your chest
and in that first instant
as you grasp "beyond"
I would presume you must let go
of the natural imagery of the river
and the green of the earth
        for that mystical
        indulgent
        darkness that remains.

PITY THE MAN
by Leon Knight

I pitied the man who wept
     from a broken heart
because a loved one died,
till
       I met a man without a heart
       who never, ever cried.

THE PLAGUE (Aids)
by Bernard V. Finney, Jr.

There is silence in the streets
and   in the churches.
The days fall away from the trees.
The dead are shadows passing by.

I am dying from the joy,
that moment,
      long forgotten
in a once sweet summer.
The light has burned out
     in my eyes
and the lesions in my throat choke songs
     I had hoped to sing.

      I leave a legacy
        of death
     for the unborn.

I cry and waste away,
     by the window
for cure and death are beyond
this room.   The door opens
     slowly;
the shadow holds my hand.

THE FUNERAL
by Bernard V. Finney, Jr.

"No siree," said Brother Joe
        sittin' on a barstool
        lookin' good for an 'ol
        man.
"I 'aint goin'
from some rundown storefront
church by da tracks wid'
no fatass woman cryin'
over da casket like dey
knows me.

I'm gonna go behin' stainglass
windas' with high chants
an smokin' candles —
sayin' goodbye

        da Episcopal way!"

MENTAL BLOCKS IN THE WEST SIDE
by Alberto O. Cappas

Pepe looked across the street
        and noticed something good
        happening in the neighborhood.
Look across the street
he told Carmen.
The building is being fixed
        up maybe now they will fix
        up the whole neighborhood.

"Que chevere"
said Carmen to Pepe.

It was the beginning of something
called gentrification moving in
        next door to all the next
        doors of the neighborhood,
            leaving no trace
            of its obvious presence.

Pepe and Carmen
        are now
very unhappily residing
        somewhere in the south bronx.

THE SAND DANCER
by Deborah A. Dessaso

shuffling
            on a four-by-four
            sprinkled with sand,
            the old man's feet
crunch
            to the tune of a jaded
            brass band

perfect rhythm,
            syncopated motion
grinding
            the grains, a black man
hoofs
            for his supper
            and a bed

KEEP THAT NIGGER RUNNIN'
by Maurice W. Britts

Once   a long time ago
I thought —
            The world's a rosy place
            full of fireworks,
            love and happiness,
            all of it just for me.
Rockets in the sky
raining bright laughter down
            on me,
kissing my cheeks
with feathery touches of love
and soft whispers —
            "Tomorrow is even better."

            That was eons ago —
sky rockets never flew.
The night remained dark
with repetitive refrain —
            "Keep that Nigger runnin'!"

TOTAL FREAK-OUT
by Beverly A. Russell

We loved our blackness
even before   Black Power

it's just that now
everyone is caught
in a   White Nightmare

MY DEADLY LOVE
by Clyde Cook

I recall
        when last I held you
        the way you eluded
                my defenses
            enslaving me
        how I loved you
            without question
                without reservation
        yearned for your
            beguiling pleasures

You promised me
        Utopia
        a dream trip through
                Eden
        gardens of delight

To possess you
        I let my life's meaning
            slip away
        I robbed and plundered
            forfeited my life
                for fantasies

Love of you
        destroyed me
        you are the devil
            in disguise
My love —
        deadly crack

HURT
by Thokozile Cox

Hurt
      that emotion almost synonomous
      with pain
a feeling
      that produces
      heat in the face
      an ache behind the eyes
accompanied by
      the breaking of the heart

hurt
      Of all emotions
      is nearly the most vivid
          second only to love
      but unlike love
hurt has not the power
      to make one both laugh
      and weep   only to cry
and experience
      a loss in a belief — forever

USED
by Maurice W. Britts

When you're young
      hope glows bright.
You are challenged
with   dreams and schemes
      to find a place
      among the stars,
called to outstrip the past,
      leave slavery's chains
        behind.

Now older,
      suddenly you see
a place among the stars
was never meant to be.
      Black leaders are used
      to keep others
      from shooting stars —
        including me.

BETRAYAL
by Nancy Ellen Webb Williams

He who lifts his
finger against his
brother should know

Destruction
must first travel
through his
own erring soul

LESS THAN SISTERS
by Ramona Wimes

You are careful in watching me.
My passion to sustain
disturbs you,
urging you to discover me
            yet know me
                    not.

You desire possession
of my gift,
            while repulsed
                    by its truth.

You gorge yourself
on stolen pieces
            of me,
without ever knowing
you do not know
me   at all.

            You failed to see
                    (when it mattered)
            we had all things
            in common.

FORGETFUL
by Cynthia Williams

You forgot
      to remember
my birthday
      in December

then
      you forgot
to remember
      me.

FOOLING OURSELVES
by Maurice W. Britts

We, don't agree on things
      We never did.
We made accommodations
      Focused on little things
That caused conflict
      Evoked rage in each other.

We don't agree on things
      We never did.
We closed out eyes
      Rosied up the passing years
Fooled ourselves
      Falsely thinking
Our lives were like all lives.

We don't agree on things
      We never did.
And with the fading years
      We came to believe
Some little precious moments
      Larger than life
Gave the illusion of agreement.

IN THE CONFINES OF HIS HOME
by William Goodin

Patiently, I watched the man, secretly
watching him not understanding —
      but I was,
as I witnessed his unique strategy
of searching for truths.

Often, he would allow himself to become
      victimized by drugs.
Sometimes, it was his reason to be weak.
Other times, it was for the hell of it.
Sometimes, it was a desire to search
      for the unknown.

He would talk about all the pains
that he had not just lived.
But in talking about his pains,
      he talked about mine.

He would cry silently (filled with pains)
as he read Marcus, King, Douglass, Brooks.
Hughs, Wright, Baldwin
      and all the unknowns
      who have struggled to contribute.
And through their tears, he found comforts
      and inspiration
      to try to make his contribution
      among the known.

He would seat himself.
He would place before him
      a cup of coffee, pencil,
      dictionary, paper
and his magical "weed."
      When he fired up,
      his thoughts would too.

DOWNTOWN
(August, 15, 1990)
by Pamela Fletcher

Downtown
in Minneapolis, Seattle, and L.A.
They sit on stoops
and stand on corners
have broken teeth
and mangled hair
and no warm beds

Downtown
in Minneapolis, Seattle, and L.A.
They sleep in shelters
where shoes are stolen
and blankets are thin
and liquor is smuggled in
where rest is seldom felt
and memories are families

Downtown
in Minneapolis, Seattle, and L.A.
at least they are friendly
so I conjure up the love they seek
in my loveless expression
and wonder about their mothers and lovers
their sisters and brothers
their fathers, children, and friends
and wonder where home really is

Downtown
in Minneapolis, Seattle, and L.A.
the streets aren't wide enough
for the black side, the brown side,
the red side, the white side
nor the yellow
and newcomers enter at their own risk
where blood is currency
passion treads lightly
and care is a four letter word

MY HOME

by Alberto O. Cappas

I have a nice apartment,
two small girls who understand innocence
            without definitions,
and a wife who doesn't understand
            my politics,
a sister-in-law who puts her two cents in
            behind my back.
I have friends who visit
            at the wrong time,
bills that drop by my mail box.
I have a father-in-law who talks to me about
            buying a house,
            starting a business
while I talk to him about
            liberation.
I have a clock that fights me every morning,
a mouse that hides from me.
(He doesn't believe me when I tell him
I, too, used to live in New York City)

I have copies of *Ramparts* at home.
They rejected my poems many times.
            Maybe I write bad poems.
I have a bad typewriter.
My girls use it when they play house.
            My wife doesn't care.
During the night after midnight,
            I read or write poetry.
In the morning the clock wakes me up,
            I am defeated by its shrill screams
My wife throws away my poems.

ABOUT THE AUTHORS

ANTONIA APOLINARIO is an African-Brazilian living in Minneapolis with her husband and two children. Writing helps her define being an immigrant in America.

HAZEL BELL, Phoenix, Arizona, is a social worker on medical retirement and a frequent contributor to Guild Press anthologies.

MARYETTA KELSICK BOOSÈ has been published extensively in poetry journals and is included in *FRAGRANT AFRICAN FLOWERS*. She is working on an autobiography, "Going About My Father's Business."

*DR. MAURICE W. BRITTS, one of the founders of Guild Press, teaches African-American literature at Metropolitan State University, St. Paul.

ALBERTO O. CAPPAS, born in Puerto Rico and now a youth worker in New York City, is included in *BLACK MEN STILL SINGING*.

*CONNEE CHIVERS-BOWMAN is a part-time teacher/tutor in the Minneapolis schools and the developer/narrator of an African-American Pioneers radio series.

*GEORGE D. CLABON, has appeared in several Guild Press anthologies, including *BLACK MEN STILL SINGING*.

BOBBY D. COBBS, born in Alabama and now living in Oakland, CA, started writing poems for his mother and grandmother at the age of ten. "I am still writing poems — thank you, Mother and Grandmother."

CLYDE COOK, New York City, says, "Illegal drug use is not the other guy's problem, it's our problem. Let's not allow gutter drugs, such as CRACK, dictate the future of our youth."

THOKOZILE COX, a scholarship student at Grinnell College, Iowa, was assistant editor of *FULL CIRCLE ELEVEN*.

ALMA CURRY, a Minneapolis poet, says, "Every teenager is my child, and I pray everyday that God will turn these current problems around."

DEBORAH A. DESSASO, a native of Washington, D.C. whose poetry has appeared in a number of publications, is being published for the first time in a Guild Press anthology.

SHIRLEY DOUGAN, born and raised in Chicago, is included in *FRAGRANT AFRICAN FLOWERS* and has helped edit several Guild Press anthologies.

BERNARD V. FINNEY, JR. is a library consultant in Albany, NY, and one of the poets in *BLACK MEN STILL SINGING*.

*PAMELA FLETCHER teaches English composition and literature courses, and is currently writing a novel about Black pioneers in Minnesota.

DARRELL GHOLAR, an alternate on the 1988 Olympic wrestling team, is currently studying theatre in Minneapolis.

*DR. RICHARD F. GILLUM, a frequent contributor to Guild Press anthologies and author of *I DONT FEEL NO WAYS TIRED*, is a medical researcher for the U.S. government.

WILLIAM GOODIN, the single parent of two boys, is one of the poets in *BLACK MEN STILL SINGING*. He hopes his truths help others overcome turmoils.

*HAZEL CLAYTON HARRISON, Pasadena, CA, is included in *FRAGRANT AFRICAN FLOWERS* and co-authored (with Ginny Knight) *A MOST DEFIANT ACT*.

CHARLENE HIGGINBOTHAM is a poet from Burnsville, MN.

BEATRICE JULIAN is a doctoral candidate in Library and Information Studies at The University of Alabama.

LAYDING LUMUMBA KALIBA, director of the Images Writers Collective of New York City and publisher of Single Action Productions, has authored several books of poetry.

*GINNY KNIGHT, artist, poet, and computer consultant in desktop publishing, edited *MURMURS OF THE PAST* and *FRAGRANT AFRICAN FLOWERS*.

*LEON KNIGHT, a poet and prose writer expelled from colonial Rhodesia in 1963, returned "home" to independent Zimbabwe in 1989. He is working on a book of short stories set in Zimbabwe and Botswana.

CHARLES E. LOVE is a composer and poet living and working in the Los Angeles area.

ERROL MILLER, Monroe, LA, has been published extensively in literary magazines since 1972. Although he is not a man of color, his poetry has universal appeal.

DORIS L. PRUITT, Houston, TX, says, "We must convince our teenagers that parenthood is an undertaking for which one must have maturity and economic stability. Otherwise, future generations will not thrive."

ELIZABETH I. ROBERTS is a widely published poet from Albany, NY.

BEVERLY RUSSELL, a librarian who lives and works in Toluca Lake, CA, is a co-author of *THREE WOMEN BLACK*.

PHYLLIS J. SLOAN, poet, editor, author of children's stories and director of a daycare center for special needs children, co-authored *THREE WOMEN BLACK* and *POSTCARD FROM HEAVEN* (children's story).

CHEMA UDE, originally from eastern Nigeria and now living in Riverside, CA, writes poetry about America, Africa and the global environment.

CYNTHIA WILLIAMS, a widely published poet, is included in *FRAGRANT AFRICAN FLOWERS*, says, "Much of my time is spent in reflection on being Black, living gray and wishing the world would forget about color."

DENNIS WILLIAMS, a Washington D.C. police officer, has been influenced as a poet by Langston Hughes, Clayde McKay and Sterling Brown.

GENE A. WILLIAMS (Sunji Ali) teaches junior high school in a "tough part" of Los Angeles and is "struggling to hone my craft — give my poetry more life and freedom."

NANCY ELLEN WEBB WILLIAMS, Las Vegas, NV, is a widely published poet who is included in *FRAGRANT AFRICAN FLOWERS*.

RAMONA WIMES is a poet currently living in Kansas City, MO.

*included in the original *ON BEING BLACK* (1981)

FULL CIRCLE SERIES

FULL CIRCLE is open to all writers and is part of an annual series of anthologies of poetry and prose (under 2,000 words).

Submission for consideration by the Editorial Committee should be mailed each year by April 1 and should include a self-addressed, stamped envelope.

Address submissions to:
FULL CIRCLE editor   P.O. Box 22583   Robbinsdale, MN 55422